Flossie Flies Home

Written by Penelope Colville Paine

Illustrated by Carl Wenzel

Paper Posie

Published by:
The Paper Posie Publishing Company
315A Meigs Road # 167, Santa Barbara, CA 93109
www.paperposie.com

ISBN 978-0-9774763-5-0

Publisher's Cataloging-in-Publication
(Provided by Quality Books, Inc.)

Paine, Penelope Colville, 1946–
    Flossie flies home / written by Penelope Colville
Paine ; illustrated by Carl Wenzel.
        pages cm
    SUMMARY: Flossie, a bee, is enticed away from her hive by a dragonfly. Alone, hungry and lost, another bee shelters Flossie. Other bees encourage her to be more assertive. Once home, she graduates to field work and is able to explain to the dragonfly that she has important work to do.
    Audience: Ages 4–8.
    LCCN 2015905863
    ISBN 978-0-9774763-5-0

    1. Bees—Juvenile fiction.   2. Assertiveness (Psychology)—Juvenile fiction. [1. Bees—Fiction. 2. Assertiveness (Psychology)—Fiction.]   I. Wenzel, Carl W., illustrator. II. Title.

PZ7.P163Flo 2015   [E]

                                              QBI15-600087

Editor: Gail Kearns   www.topressandbeyond.com   /
Typography: Cirrus Book Design

Printed in China, Shenzhen, Guangdong
08/2015, C&C Printing Company, Ltd.
10   9   8   7   6   5   4   3   2   1

Special thanks to Cathy Feldman, Philip Davidson and Paul Cronshaw

*For all my hardworking
honeybee sisters.*

This year the bees had been very busy.
The Honey Store was open and visitors were
buying jars of honey.

Flossie, one of the bees, was resting on a rose near the Honey Store. "Phew," she sighed, "my wings are tired from fanning the air in the hive."

"Can't let the air get too hot," another bee said. "It's an important job."

Flossie had other jobs to learn. Last week she helped take care of the baby bees. Tomorrow she had to be a guard and make sure strangers stayed away from the hive.

Flossie had LOTS of sisters. They told her exciting stories about going into the fields. "One day you will learn the waggle dance and be able to give directions, then you will become a worker bee," they said.

Flossie and her sister guards took turns flying around the garden, making sure the hive was safe. "Be careful not to go over the fence," an older sister advised. Soon Flossie knew every corner of the garden. Sometimes she and her sisters turned somersaults to entertain the children at the Honey Store.

One afternoon, Flossie was startled by a loud hum.

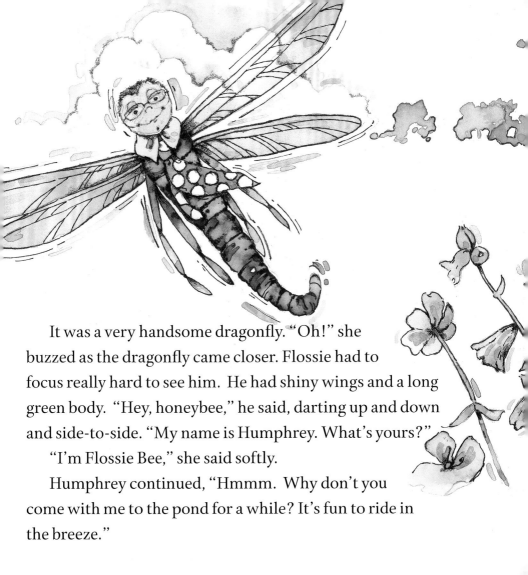

It was a very handsome dragonfly. "Oh!" she buzzed as the dragonfly came closer. Flossie had to focus really hard to see him. He had shiny wings and a long green body. "Hey, honeybee," he said, darting up and down and side-to-side. "My name is Humphrey. What's yours?"

"I'm Flossie Bee," she said softly.

Humphrey continued, "Hmmm. Why don't you come with me to the pond for a while? It's fun to ride in the breeze."

"I'm on guard," she explained. "I have to get back to work. I'm not supposed to go over the fence."

"Come on, you'll love it," Humphrey insisted. "No one will miss you!"

Flossie wanted to have fun. "Okay," she said, "but just for a little while."

"Great," Humphrey said. "You can meet my friends." Flossie followed him up into the sky.

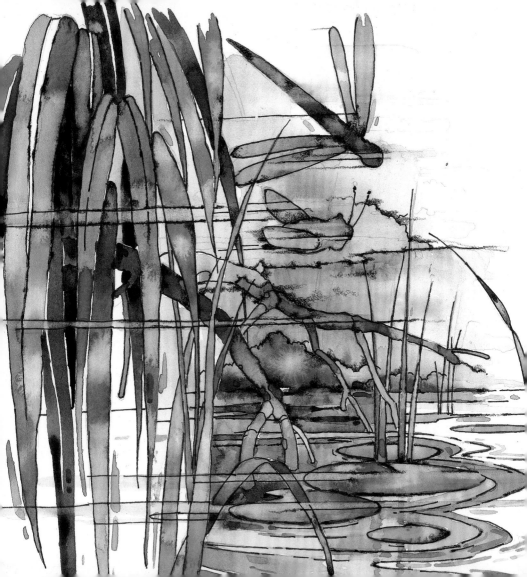

Soon they were under big willow trees by a shady pond. "Hey guys," Humphrey called to his pals. "Come and meet Miss Flossie Bee." The dragonflies zigzagged over to Flossie. "Hmmm," they hummed loudly, looking at her with their big eyes.

Showing off, Humphrey dove in and out of the water. He was very good at flying. But after a while, some gnats caught his attention, and he flew away.

Flossie was suddenly alone. She looked for some flowers because she was getting hungry. All she could find were ferns and reeds. This was not a place for bees!

Seeing a thin ray of sunlight, she flew toward the
light, hoping to find her sisters so that she could follow
them home across the fields. But Flossie was heading
for the main road.

The main road was noisy, and the air was bad. Flossie found it hard to breathe. A big truck roared by. The wind blew her along so fast that she couldn't make her wings work. Before she knew what was happening, Flossie was blown through a car window.

"Look out! It's a bee!" A woman shouted, waving a rolled up newspaper in the air.

Frantically, Flossie looked for somewhere to hide.

She spotted some flowers on the woman's hat and flew under a petal. The flowers were stiff and scratchy, not like the flowers she knew. They had no pollen or nectar, not even a smell.

Eventually, the car stopped. "Here we are," the woman said, opening the car door as Flossie clung to the petal.

When Flossie peeked out she saw lots more people. She needed to escape, so she used her last ounce of strength to fly away.

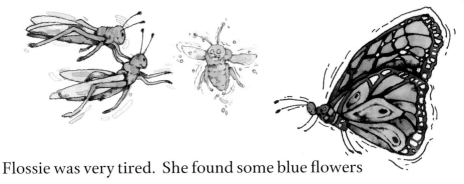

Flossie was very tired. She found some blue flowers and hungrily sucked the nectar.

Now she had to find her way home. "Oh dear," she thought. "I wish I knew the waggle dance, the one my sisters told me about.

Looking around she noticed a fly. "Excuse me," she asked politely, "do you know the way to my hive?"

"What'd you say?" he answered rudely, bumping into a flower.

A beautiful butterfly stopped to fan her wings. "Could you help me?" Flossie asked. But the butterfly just fluttered away.

And when Flossie wiggled around hoping some grasshoppers might understand her, they thought it was a huge joke and leapt right over her head into the field.

Just as she was about to give up, a bee came by.

"Oh, you poor dear," the bee said, noticing Flossie. "You are not one of my sisters. Have you lost your way?" Flossie nodded. "It's okay," the bee comforted her. "I can help. Come back to my hive."

The bee led her over the crest of the hill and into a big field.

Flossie was so heavy from all the pollen that she could hardly keep up.

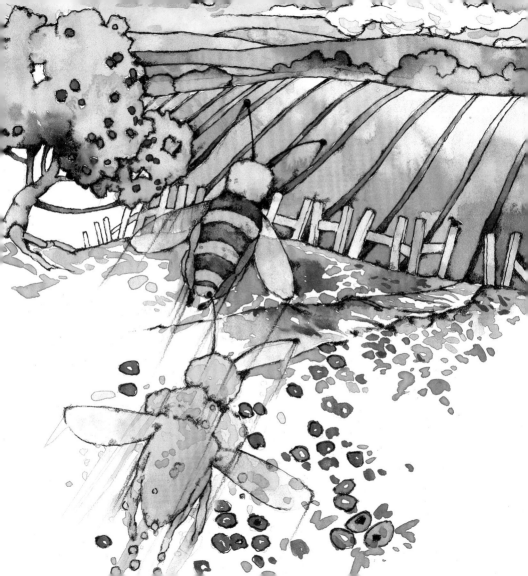

The hive was like Flossie's—warm and sweet smelling. When the guards saw that she was not going to steal their honey, they made her feel welcomed and helped her find a spot to rest for the night. "How did you get here?" they asked.

Flossie told her story. Those dragonflies," they laughed. "They just want to play all day, but we have work to do. Next time, Flossie, you just tell that Humphrey to buzz off." They all practiced buzzing very loudly until one of the older bees asked them to be quiet.

"I think I know where your hive is," one of the bees said. "When the sun is up we will give you directions."

In the morning several bees took Flossie over to the main road and showed her how to avoid the cars and which way to fly. Soon she found one of her own sisters, and she followed her back to her hive.

"Flossie, where were you? Why did you go away?" her sisters asked, crowding around. Flossie was embarrassed as she told her story. "Well, we missed you, and we are glad you are back. It is summer, and we have lots to do!" They all gave her a tickly bee hug. "Then we're all going to visit the fireflies after work." Flossie felt much better. "Quick, let's go," a bee said. They all flew off, leaving Flossie on guard duty again.

Just before dusk, Flossie and her sisters flew over to the oak tree. The crickets were striking up a chord, the fireflies were dancing, and she and her sisters chased the moths. Soon it was time to rest and get ready for the next day's work.

Flossie was excited. Tomorrow she was going to join her worker bee sisters in the fields.

Flossie stayed close to a sister as they flew back and forth. There was no fence to follow, only the open fields. She had to perfect her waggle dance to give and receive directions. She had to learn the landmarks. Sometimes, she would take a quick spin around the store where she had grown up. "Keep up the good work!" the storeowner called out.

One morning, Flossie heard a rather loud hum near the daisies. It was Humphrey again. "Hello, Humphrey," she said. She remembered what she and her friends had practiced. "You were very rude the other day, flying away and leaving me alone. I thought I would never get home, and if it wasn't for my friends," she quivered, "I don't know where I'd be right now."

Flossie went on, "Please don't bother me again Humphrey! I have important things to do."

For once Humphrey was still, and his eyes were wide in amazement. He had never met anyone like Flossie. Without a word he turned and flew away.

When they saw Flossie with Humphrey, several sisters called out, "Are you coming home, Flossie?"

"Yes!" Flossie buzzed happily, flying toward the hive, "I'm coming home!"